THE ONLY

VISION BOARD

CLIP ART BOOK

--- you'll ever need ---

by
Gloria Greene

VISION BOARD TIPS FOR LIFE-CHANGING MANIFESTATION

01 Be specific and clear about your goals and intentions, and choose images and affirmations that align with these intentions.

02 Select images that truly resonate with you and represent your desired outcomes. These images should evoke positive emotions and inspire you to take action towards achieving your goals.

03 Hang your board somewhere prominent where you will see it several times a day, e.g. by the kettle in the kitchen.

04 Incorporate positive affirmations that align with your intentions and goals. These affirmations should be uplifting and empowering, and should help to reinforce your positive mindset.

05 Every morning, choose one image, close your eyes and imagine how you will feel when it comes true. Transport yourself into the moment and allow yourself to feel like you have it already.

Say YES to NEW ADVENTURES

✈ UNIVERSAL AIRLINES

Boarding Pass

Boarding Pass

Passenger Name

Flight
AB 1234

Seat
15A

Passenger Name

From

To

Date

Gate
A5

From

To

Boarding Time
10:00 AM

Flight
AB 1234

Seat
15A

Gate
A5

0 1 2 3 4 5 6 7 8 9

Boarding Time
10:00 AM

✈ UNIVERSAL AIRLINES

Boarding Pass

Boarding Pass

Passenger Name

Flight
AB 1234

Seat
15A

Passenger Name

From

To

Date

Gate
A5

From

To

Boarding Time
10:00 AM

Flight
AB 1234

Seat
15A

Gate
A5

0 1 2 3 4 5 6 7 8 9

Boarding Time
10:00 AM

✈ UNIVERSAL AIRLINES

Boarding Pass

Boarding Pass

Passenger Name

Flight
AB 1234

Seat
15A

Passenger Name

From

To

Date

Gate
A5

From

To

Boarding Time
10:00 AM

Flight
AB 1234

Seat
15A

Gate
A5

0 1 2 3 4 5 6 7 8 9

Boarding Time
10:00 AM

✈ UNIVERSAL AIRLINES

Boarding Pass

Boarding Pass

Passenger Name

Flight
AB 1234

Seat
15A

Passenger Name

From

To

Date

Gate
A5

From

To

Boarding Time
10:00 AM

Flight
AB 1234

Seat
15A

Gate
A5

0 1 2 3 4 5 6 7 8 9

Boarding Time
10:00 AM

mexico

BRAZIL

Australia

Greece

ITALY

SPAIN

Thailand

SOUTH AFRICA

new zealand

Japan

india

FRANCE

EUROPE

MOSCOW

BALI

Ireland

morocco

Croatia

Scotland

maldives

ROME

CUBA

VANCOUVER

Dubai

Bora Bora

Los Angeles

new york

Singapore

I am attracting a partner who loves and accepts me for who I am

I am excited to create a beautiful future with the partner of my dreams, filled with love, laughter, and joy.

love

I am releasing any past hurt or negative patterns that may have blocked me from love.

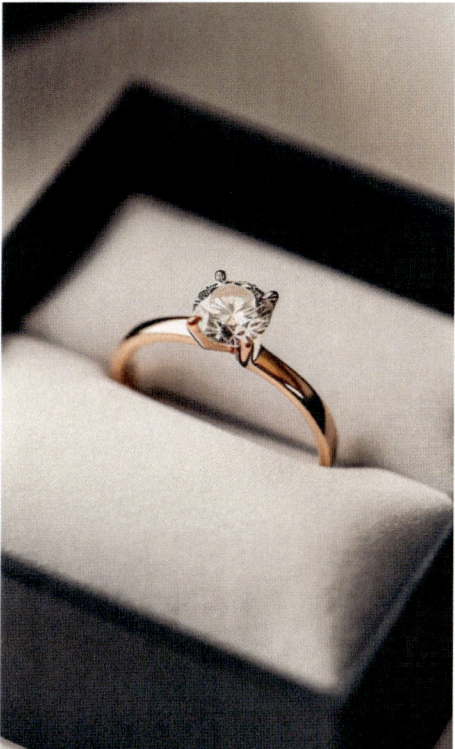

Certificate of Marriage

This Certifies that

_____ and _____

were united in marriage on

_____

wedding

My mind and body are open and ready to receive a new life

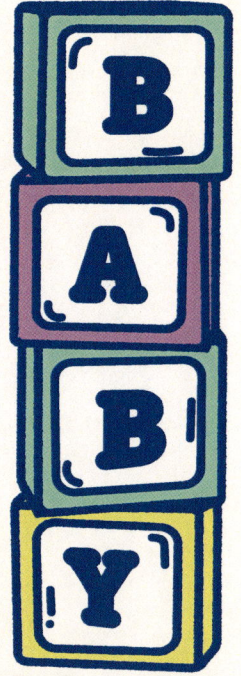

BABY

I trust my body and it's ability to conceive a healthy baby

GENERAL HOSPITAL
Certificate of Birth

This Certifies that_____

weight _____ lbs. _____ oz. was born in this Hospital

on the _____ day of _____

In Witness Whereof this Certificate has been duly signed by the Happy Parents.

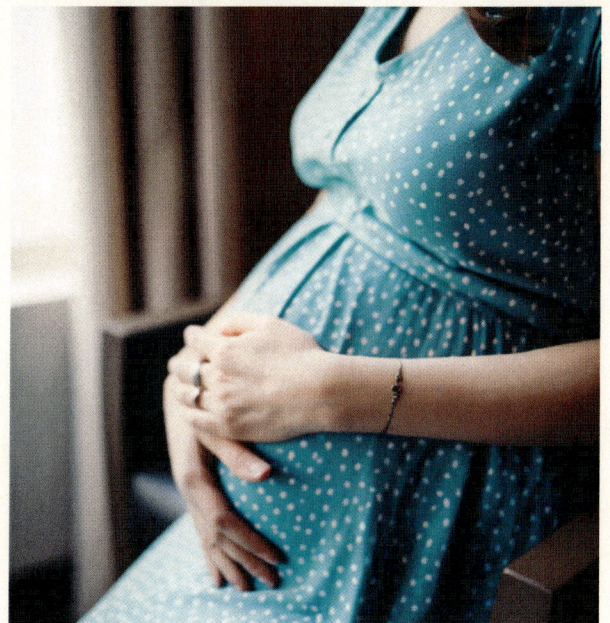

_____

PARENTS

I am grateful for my family, who loves and supports me <u>unconditionally</u>.

FAMILY TIME

My family is a gift from the UNIVERSE, and I am thankful for their presence in my life.

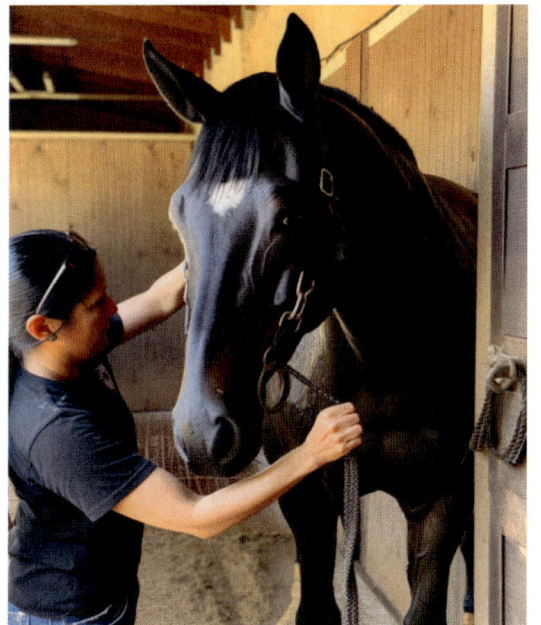

ART

PROMOTION

INFLUENCER

INVESTMENTS

ABUNDANCE

LUXURY CRUISE

FORGIVE

WRITE A BOOK

SEE THE WORLD

New Wheels

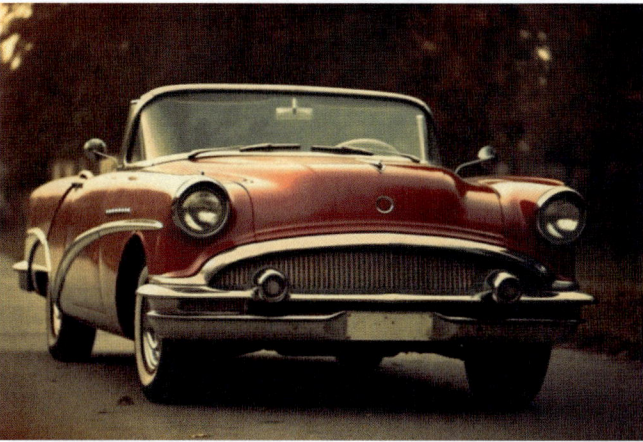

DRIVER LICENSE

Name

D.O.B

OFFICIAL

Certificate of Graduation

awarded to

for

_____    _____

Date   Signature

SUCCESS

YOUTUBER

CONFIDENCE

adventure

HAPPINESS

authenticity

GRATITUDE

FREEDOM

GROWTH

AMBITION

DREAMS

INSPIRATION

COURAGE

CAREER →

Start your side hustle

I am confident in my abilities

DESIGNER CLOTHING

LUXURY VILLA

FINANCIAL FREEDOM

DEBT FREE

MORTGAGE FREE

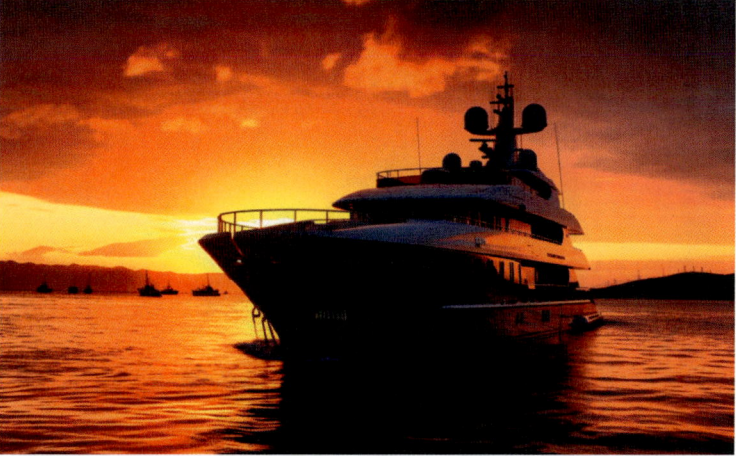

I am grateful for the financial abundance that flows into my life

I attract abundance and wealth into my life effortlessly and easily

BANK OF THE UNIVERSE

Date: _____

Pay: _____

_____

_____ Dollars

$

The Universe

AUTHORIZED SIGNATURE

0123456 789 87654321   0123456 789 87654321

BANK OF THE UNIVERSE

Date: _____

Pay: _____

_____

_____ Dollars

$

The Universe

AUTHORIZED SIGNATURE

0123456 789 87654321   0123456 789 87654321

BANK OF THE UNIVERSE

Date: _____

Pay: _____

_____

_____ Dollars

$

The Universe

AUTHORIZED SIGNATURE

0123456 789 87654321   0123456 789 87654321

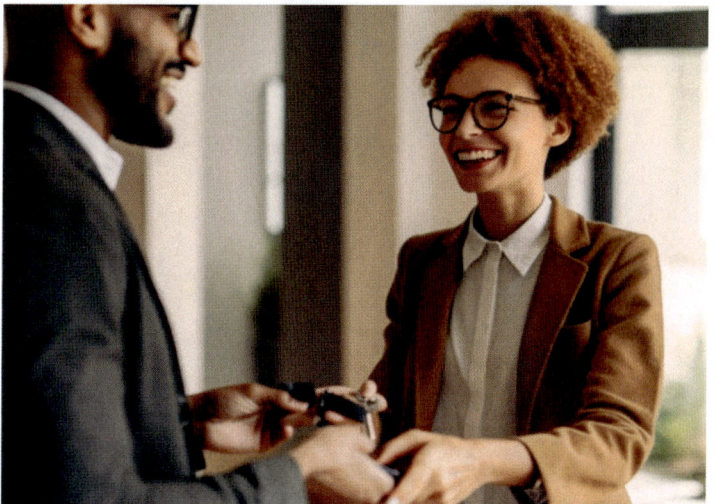

I am proud of myself for taking this big step towards financial stability and independence.

I am grateful for my new home, and I am excited to create many happy memories here.

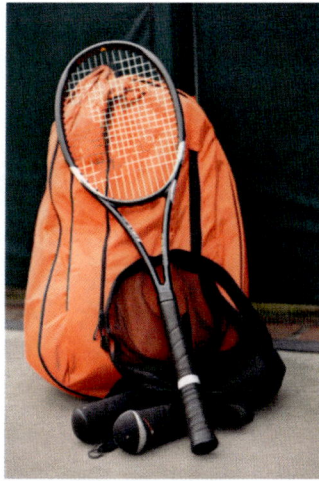

I AM STRONG

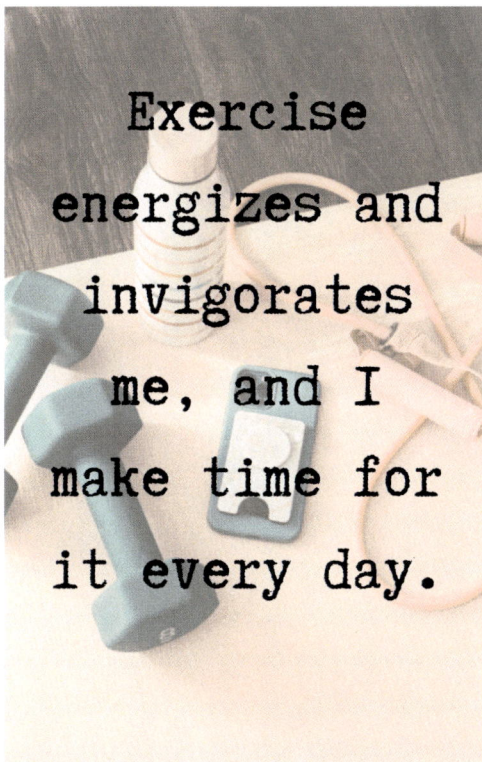

Exercise energizes and invigorates me, and I make time for it every day.

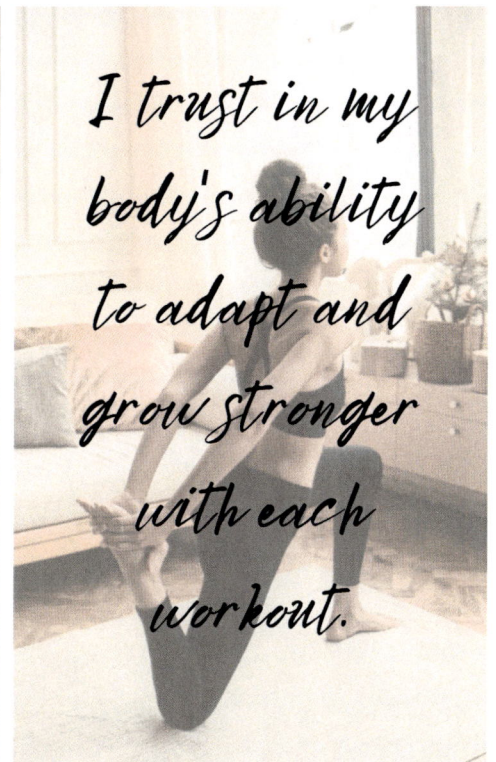

I trust in my body's ability to adapt and grow stronger with each workout.

Lose

Pounds

FRIENDSHIP

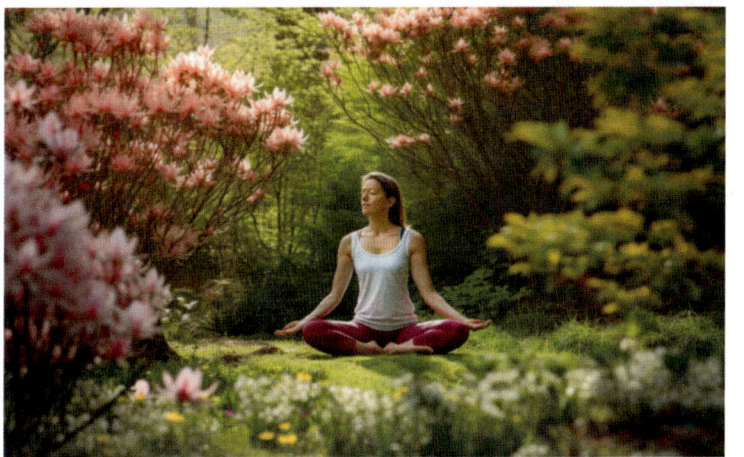

Making time for my hobbies is essential to my overall well-being and happiness

GOALS

REWARDING CAREER

LOVING RELATIONSHIP

LOSE WEIGHT

DREAM VACATION

FAMILY TIME

FITNESS

TRAVEL

HEALTH

NEW CAR

SELF CARE

spirituality

GRADUATION

FAMILY

wealth

home

baby

CAREER

relationship

DO MORE EXERCISE

NEW HOME

SOULMATE

DRIVERS LICENCE

DE-STRESS

$1,000,000

READ MORE

MEDITATE

ME TIME

TREASURE LOVE Breathe

magic SOUL Spiritual

FOCUSED

magical *I am strong* read

Heal SHARING INTUITION

REST, RELAX CAREER My place

Weekend away self-care PEACE

RECHARGE THANKFUL Acceptance

Perspective FRIEND mighty

Eat well thrive FOREVER Soul

HEALTH Creative happier

FEELINGS I am enough SLEEP BETTER

DON'T STRESS Self-compassion TRUST

happiness

TRUE CALLING

RITUALS

Confidence

NEW DIRECTION

nurtured

visualise

pampering

move forward

transition

Meditation

Clarity

Hope

GOALS

WALK

POWERFUL

HEAL

HAPPY

self-compassion

CONFIDENT

positive

Learning

I am succeeding

I am loved

success

intimacy.

New beginnings

ENERGY

Hey there!

We just wanted to take a moment to say thank you for choosing our vision board book. We hope it's helping you manifest your dreams and inspiring you to be the best version of yourself.

If you're loving the book, we'd be over the moon if you could leave us a review on Amazon. It helps us out so much, and we appreciate it more than you know.

Also, we have other books that we think you'll love too! Check out our collection of Vision Board titles at www.amazon.com/author/gloriagreene, or scan this QR code.

Learn how to use the power of positive thinking and visualization to manifest your goals and desires with this FREE eBook.

FREE E-BOOK

THE VISION BOARD
By Gloria Greene

Harnessing the Power of the Law of Attraction to Achieve Your Goals

Scan this QR code to download your FREE eBook.

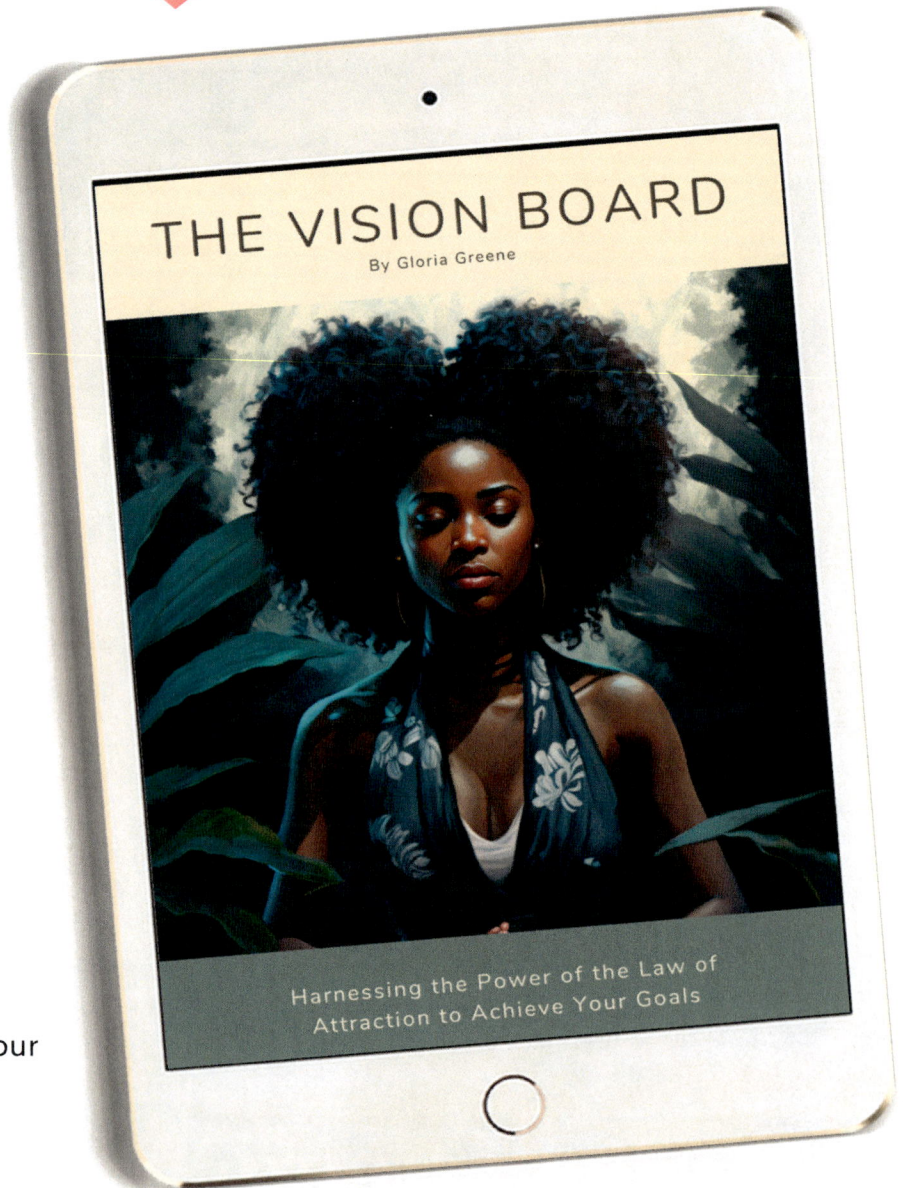

Made in the USA
Coppell, TX
11 December 2023